Let Go Or Be Dragged Again

nancy delong

Let Go Or Be Dragged Again

Written by
Nancy DeLong

Edited by
Amy Bouwer

Designed by
Jason Carey

© 2022 Nancy DeLong
ISBN: 978-1-941320-21-1
Printed in the United States of America
First Edition, First Printing

Published by N. Glynn Publishing, LLC
Lake Mary, FL 32746

All rights reserved. No portion of this book may be reproduced, stored in a retrieval system, or transmitted in any form or by any means, without the expressed written permission of the publisher. However, a reviewer may quote brief passages in a review to be printed in a newspaper, magazine, journal, or any appropriate electronic means.

nancydelong.com

N. GLYNN PUBLISHING, LLC

To those who have shown love and kindness to another instead of judgement; to those who have met a challenge, struggled, fallen, and courageously gotten up; to those who have listened instead of clamoring to be heard; to all of you, I dedicate this book.

The long awaited sequel, *Let Go Or Be Dragged Again*, is a collection of new affirmations for living in harmony one day at a time. Each day we make a choice to breathe in joy, love, and laughter or to be dragged. May this book give you the encouragement to "let go" and embrace your stunning life.

For years, I heard people say, "Let go and let God." It always sounded like someone was flapping pancakes. It was annoying. One day, I realized that for me, when I did not let go, I was being dragged. "Let Go or Be Dragged" resonates for me.

As you hold this book in your hands, feel the love energy it holds. As you read a page, feel joy. When you come to a day with a very short saying, let it speak to the place in your heart that you have yet to honor. As you read a longer passage, may it stir passion inside of you. This book is meant to be a personal experience outside of the words on the page. The words are merely the starting point of your journey into the cosmos of your original intentionality.

At the end of the day, you only have two choices. You must choose to either let go or be dragged. Sometimes it is a monumental decision. My wish is that this book inspires you to welcome the life-changing opportunity to "let go."

25 JULY
DAY OUT OF TIME

Calendars were invented to measure time so our human brains would not explode. The 400-year-old Gregorian Calendar, used today, is based on the solar cycle of Earth. For eons, people used the Mayan calendar based on the lunar cycle. There was an extra day between the last day of the year and the first. This was called the "Day Out of Time."

More recently, this day has been reignited with ceremonies dedicated to artistic expression and creativity. It is a day to pause and breathe, to practice universal forgiveness, to reflect on the past, and welcome the future. What a magnificent time to be aware!

Today, I step out of my ordinary reality into the tenth dimension where time is art. Today, I feel the timelessness and freedom of being perfectly alive. Today, I close my eyes and embrace this Day Out of Time. Today, I choose to let go.

july

26 JULY
First Day

Being conscious of an Omnipotent Essence, whatever you believe it to be, is the beginning of letting go.

27 JULY

"We" is the magic word of all of humanity. We need each other, we need to listen to each other, we need to encourage and lift up each other; but most of all, we need to LOVE one each other.

28 JULY

"At this time in history, we are to take nothing personally, least of all ourselves. For the moment that we do, our spiritual growth and journey comes to a halt."
~Hopi Elder, Oraibi, Arizona

29 JULY

Be true to yourself first. You can only nurture and help others by first honoring your original intentionality.

30 JULY

What an awesome time to be alive! We are being called to action to protect our democracy. Standing together, we are willing to pay the price to reclaim our freedom.

31 JULY

Since your actions reflect who you really are, show kindness to unkind people, forgive people who don't deserve it, and love unconditionally.

august

1 AUGUST

"Never speak of others in a mean way. The negative energy you put out into the Universe is going to multiply when it returns to you."
~Native American Code of Ethics, 1994

2 AUGUST

"Live in harmony with formless intelligence, which is always creative and never competitive in spirit!" chirped the meadowlark.

Thinking of you, John Sinclair

3 AUGUST

My purpose is to be of service to others. In order to do that, I must have peace of mind.

4 AUGUST

Less than ideal can still be amazing. Here's a news flash: Life is mostly less than ideal, but it can always, always be amazing.

5 AUGUST

Joy is being who you really are and becoming all that you are capable of becoming.

6 AUGUST

Opportunities are everywhere. They are especially abundant in those places that people rarely frequent. Hmmm, that's interesting.

7 AUGUST

Happiness ~ some pursue it, others create it.

8 AUGUST

Today, may I live in the anointing of the Holy Spirit instead of going on my own wind.

9 AUGUST

One of the most calming and powerful actions you take to intervene in a stormy world is to stand up and show your soul.

Happy Birthday, Liam Reed Spires

10 AUGUST

Happiness is a journey rather than a goal. It is a daily experience of seeing the beauty around you, embracing the experiences of the day without judgement, and knowing that you are brushing up against the grace of a power far greater than anything you can even imagine.

I love you Mom, Happy Birthday!

11 AUGUST

"The soul would have no rainbow if the eyes had no tears."

~Native American Proverb

12 AUGUST

Today be enthusiastic! It will always, always make you feel better.

13 AUGUST

What is your number one priority today? Does your heart back that up? Does your checkbook back that up? Does your calendar back that up? If not, why not?

14 AUGUST

"What you meet in another being is the projection of your own level of evolution."

~Ram Dass

15 AUGUST

The key to immortality is creating a loving impact on the lives of those around you. You will forever occupy a place in their hearts and minds. In turn, they will pass on a little piece of you as they touch the lives of others. Imagine that!

Happy Birthday, Jessica Horne

16 AUGUST

Be part of a pocket of enthusiasm today! It will change the world.

Thinking of you, Leo DiSabato

17 AUGUST

"When you finally let people love you exactly the way they do, it's pretty easy to see that's all they've ever been trying to do the whole time."
~StoryPeople

18 AUGUST

Today, astonish a mean world with stunning acts of kindness!

19 AUGUST

"What is life? It is the flash of a firefly in the night. It is the breath of a buffalo in the winter time. It is the little shadow that runs across the grass and loses itself in the sunset."
~Crowfoot, Blackfoot Lakota

Happy Birthday, Pampy Old Boy

20 AUGUST

I can only be as honest as I am aware, and once I become aware, I become accountable for my actions.

21 AUGUST

"Anyone can slay a dragon," she told me, "but try waking up every morning & loving the world all over again. That's what takes a real hero."
~StoryPeople

22 AUGUST

God's grace is available to everyone on the planet. It brings us together in love; it sustains us in every moment. Our part is to ask for this gift of grace. Oh, and one more thing, it's a daily request. So, ask today and tomorrow and every day.

23 AUGUST

Feel the grace of living in conscious contact rather than conscious separation.

24 AUGUST

You are the spiritual healer of you. When you believe your healing comes from any Earth source outside of you, then you're sadly mistaken.

Thinking of you, Michel Reed

25 AUGUST

When people move on, let them. Room is being made for new people to come into your life bringing joy and laughter.

26 AUGUST

"We weaken our greatness when we confuse our patriotism with tribal rivalries that have sown resentment and hatred and violence in all the corners of the globe. We weaken it when we hide behind walls rather than tear them down, when we doubt the power of our ideals rather than trust them to be the great force for change they have always been."
~United States Senator John McCain

27 AUGUST

"Happiness increases the more you spread it around."
~Unknown

28 AUGUST

Life is meant to break us open so our hearts can be free!

29 AUGUST

Mindfulness is the psychological process of bringing one's attention to experiences occurring in the present moment. Simply put, live in the moment today and tomorrow and the day after that.

30 AUGUST

It's hard to hate up close. It's time to be warmhearted to everyone you meet. Think about it.

31 AUGUST

"Looking for consciousness inside the brain is like looking inside a radio for the announcer."
~Nassim Haramein

september

1 SEPTEMBER

Words are so powerful and revealing. Whether you write them or speak them, choose words carefully today. A single word can change your intended meaning. So say what you mean, and mean what you say.

2 SEPTEMBER

There are moments in our lives that change our trajectory forever. Sometimes we know instantly; sometimes we look back with gentle reflection and smile.

3 SEPTEMBER

"Technology's potential is, and always must be, rooted in the faith people have in it, in the optimism and the creativity that it stirs in the hearts of individuals, and in its promise and capacity to make the world a better place."
~Tim Cook, CEO, Apple, Inc.

4 SEPTEMBER

In today's world, people do not know what action to take because they have no context. Lack of context is our dilemma, not lack of information.

Thinking of you, Jason Carey

5 SEPTEMBER

We are living in a new energy flow. We need to be mature enough to see the light and meet this new energy head-on.

6 SEPTEMBER

The spiritual connection between two of God's kids comes through grace.

7 SEPTEMBER

Whether you are going through a hurricane or a pandemic, protect your loved ones, be kind to everyone who crosses your path, and take only what you need. Remember, together we are resilient.

8 SEPTEMBER

What if this was the day the Holy Mother Mary, Jesus' mom, was born. How would we celebrate? Would we have a party with family and friends? Would we bake a cake? Whatever we would do, it would be a Love Fest because that was the message that came to Earth through Mary. It has been said in many ways, but its meaning never changes. Love One Another! Oh, that's worth celebrating every day.

Thinking of you, Jesse James Pope

9 SEPTEMBER

One of the reasons that talk is cheap is because the supply far exceeds the demand.

10 SEPTEMBER

Today, I will share joy with others just for the fun of it!

11 SEPTEMBER

Releasing grief is a process. We humans grieve the loss of the people who disappear from our lives. We grieve changes, even when the changes are for the better. We grieve the experiences in our lives when we have felt hurt or lost. We are told to "get over it," and that never works. We do not truly "get over" anything unless we go through it and feel the grief. So, breathe through your grief today, whatever it may be. And if you don't think your are holding on to grief, you're lying to yourself.

12 SEPTEMBER

The power of prayer is above reproach, so I pray for your highest good and greatest purpose, and I leave the rest to God.

13 SEPTEMBER

You will change the energy on the planet when you find your calling and do your best to be of service. So, do that today.

14 SEPTEMBER

You wonder what it would be like to be loved for everything you are & I want to take your face in my hands & say, "You already are. Now, you just have to remember to feel it."
~StoryPeople

Thinking of you, Amy Bouwer

15 SEPTEMBER

I think I know what I don't know. So today, I pray to set aside everything I think I know about anything and ask God to intervene. Now, I will listen.

16 SEPTEMBER

We are living in a time when, more than ever before, community must be embraced and nourished. Find your like-minded earthlings and celebrate!

17 SEPTEMBER

Whenever we approach anything in our lives with contempt prior to investigation, we limit our opportunities to grow.

18 SEPTEMBER

Slowly is the fastest way to get to where you want to be. Hmmm, maybe, maybe not.

19 SEPTEMBER

Lovingly listening to others is more useful than trying to make them change to your way of thinking.

20 SEPTEMBER

No matter what is happening in your life today remember this: What you think is a catastrophe, God turns into a treasure.

21 SEPTEMBER

Our spiritual connection helps us face the music even when we don't like the tune.

22 SEPTEMBER

Create your life by deliberate design, by positive thoughts, and with a loving heart.

23 SEPTEMBER

When you're in a dark place, and it feels like you've been buried, you've actually been planted.

Thinking of you, Polly Pistole

24 SEPTEMBER

People will say what they will say about you, but your friends know the truth of you.

25 SEPTEMBER

When we are inspired, we learn; when we are passionate, we achieve.

26 SEPTEMBER

"When the world seems to be on a self-destructive path, find hope and success. Allow your past to inform you, rather than dictate to you. Then hope will come more easily," said the mighty oak.

27 SEPTEMBER

Believe that you were born under a very bright star and see how that changes the projection of your life.

Happy Birthday Jill Spires

28 SEPTEMBER

The bars of the strongest prison known to man are made up of the opinions other people have of us. Think about it.

29 SEPTEMBER

The Universe shouts, "Stop being a victim. Stop thinking you have to do it right. There is no right or wrong, only experiences. Your part is to feel it, gain from the experience, and move forward with a bag of tools to help others."

30 SEPTEMBER

Here's a test. Review how you've spent your resources in the past month. How did you spend your time? How did you spend your money? Who did you spend it with? What actions did you take each day toward your goals? When you answer these questions, you will become clear about the direction of your life. This is true, whether you think these are your goals and priorities or not. So, if your vision for your life is something different, change your daily actions and repeat them, over and over and over again. Do it now.

october

1 OCTOBER

Your heart is never wrong, ever. Listen to it!

2 OCTOBER

"The time for the lone wolf is over. Gather yourselves! Banish the word 'struggle' from your attitude and your vocabulary. All that we do now must be done in a sacred manner and in celebration. We are the ones we've been waiting for."

~Hopi Elder, Oraibi, Arizona

Happy Birthday to me!

3 OCTOBER

Sometimes the bravest thing a person can do is be himself in an intimate relationship. It puts everything on the table from possibility to rejection. The problem is that we often fear rejection so much that we close our hearts and become a reflection of the person we are with.

4 OCTOBER

There is an abundance of joy in the universe and a limited amount of pain. So today, swim in joy!

5 OCTOBER

"When a person comes into your life who inspires you, you take notice."

~StoryPeople

Happy Birthday, Sophie Jump

6 OCTOBER

When I decide to open my heart to the world, I choose to accept vulnerability, empathy, and sensitivity as strengths. When I can trust the feelings of love, openness, and acceptance, I feel immense power in my life, one that exceeds my physical limitations.

7 OCTOBER

Thoughts matter. Believe it or not, like it or not. It is always, always the truth.

8 OCTOBER

Only you can write your story, so never, ever buy into anyone else's version of you.

9 OCTOBER

My memories are the stories I've been telling myself about the past, and they may or may not be true.

10 OCTOBER

To be effective and useful, we have to be awake to the energy around us and to be spiritually connected to it. We are all part of the energy of one.

11 OCTOBER

When we know we are part of everything, we honor everything in our path.

12 OCTOBER

So often we look at the events in our lives as we want them to be rather than the way they actually are. See the real reality today and fully live in it. Remember, this is a daily task.

13 OCTOBER

"Imperfection is beauty, madness is genius, and it's better to be absolutely ridiculous than absolutely boring."

~Marilyn Monroe

14 OCTOBER

Sound vibration restores health. Sound vibration moving through water restores the soul.

15 OCTOBER

I stopped explaining myself the day I realized that people only understand from their level of perception. They cannot hear what they cannot hear.

16 OCTOBER

Listening with my third ear is my loving action which dissolves any dis-ease, anger, or resentment I am harboring.

Thinking of you, Rena Keene

17 OCTOBER

Some things make us hard and soft at the same time. Think about it!

18 OCTOBER

The decisions you make, the actions you take in this moment will affect the quality of your future.

19 OCTOBER

Without words, there are no songs. Without songs, there are no tunes. Oh, but there is always music!

20 OCTOBER

Believe in yourself and your own power to heal and transform the world from hatred into love.

21 OCTOBER

What if the only thing the Essence of Love wants for me is to be joy-filled today. My part is to open my heart and receive it.

22 OCTOBER

Laugh today! Laughter raises your spirit and connects you to the abundant joy of the Universe.

23 OCTOBER

"The most important aspect of love is not in the giving or the receiving; it's in the being."
~Ram Dass

24 OCTOBER

Today, I am cooperating with God by being in his presence, believing that he has my back, showing kindness to everyone I meet, doing my part with a happy heart, and belly laughing often.

Thinking of you, Sue Jones

25 OCTOBER

As long as my steps are in alignment with my intention, these will take me to my desire, want, and purpose. But first, I must have the clarity of my intention.

26 OCTOBER

Mindfulness is the psychological process of bringing one's attention to experiences occurring in the present moment. This sounds like a simple concept, but it takes a lot of practice. So today practice like this: Pause. Pray. Proceed. Now watch how your world changes.

27 OCTOBER

DNA is a frequency made of light. Think about it. Oh, this changes everything!

28 OCTOBER

"I will carry you with me to the end of my days, remembering all the moments you taught me to trust my own heart to be alive."
~StoryPeople

Thinking of you, Dad

29 OCTOBER

Enthusiasm without direction is like running at top speed through the forest in the dark.

30 OCTOBER

God, please remove my fear today and direct me to what you would have me be. May I do your will always.

31 OCTOBER

"Discerning is what love allows. It binds people together but holds them separate so they can know themselves," hooted the owl.

Thinking of you, Leslie John Rafferty

november

1 NOVEMBER

"I promise you not a moment will be lost as long as I have heart & voice to speak & we will walk again together with a thousand others & a thousand more & on & on until there is no one among us who does not know the truth: there is no future without love."
~StoryPeople

Thinking of you, Otto Budig

2 NOVEMBER

"There was a time when the land was sacred, and the ancient ones were at one with it. It was a time when only the children of Great Spirit were here to light their fires in these places with no boundaries. In that time, when there were only simple ways, I saw with my heart the conflicts to come, and whether it was to be for good or bad, what was certain was that there would be change," whispered the wind.

3 NOVEMBER

Everything is energy! So whether it's a star or a bird or a rainbow or you, it's all the same stuff.

4 NOVEMBER

True friendship is the light in the window on a dark night.

5 NOVEMBER

Today, trust Great Spirit to guide your actions and to take you one step closer to your wildest dreams. Trust this even when you do not trust yourself.

Happy Birthday, Jenny Jump

6 NOVEMBER

In the midst of chaos, the truth can still shine through. As we return to harmony, something can be learned and shared. You ask, "How is harmony restored?" The answer lies within you.

7 NOVEMBER

Future elections will be won by heart connections, not head connections.

8 NOVEMBER

Fear is an evil threat to humanity. Remember this before you act in anger because all anger masks fear.

9 NOVEMBER

Sometimes we say the things we really need to hear. Wow!

10 NOVEMBER

Today is an opportunity to blend your energies with those around you, and share your gifts and insights.

11 NOVEMBER

May your heart overflow with the love from within you!

12 NOVEMBER

When you think something is too hard, remember that it's supposed to be hard. If it weren't, everyone would be doing it.

13 NOVEMBER

Light is everything. Since love and light are the same stuff, when we become aware of this, healing can begin. Hmmm, now "All We Need is Love" makes sense. Let your brain get around that today.

14 NOVEMBER

Today is the tomorrow you worried about yesterday. And the moral to this statement is: Be in the moment!

15 NOVEMBER

I find my peace when I am in the realm of God. And, the realm of God exists only in one place ~ the present moment.

16 NOVEMBER

Kindness lives deep within your soul; breathe through the barriers that are standing in the way of showing your kindness to the world.

Happy Birthday, John Jump & Chuck Little

17 NOVEMBER

Be amazed by the love and joy in your life today.

18 NOVEMBER

"Knowledge is only rumor until it lives in your bones."
~Asaro Tribe, Papua, New Guinea

19 NOVEMBER

Spread the love today. Think about it, feel it. Believe me, it matters.

20 NOVEMBER

The soul needs only meaning to thrive.

21 NOVEMBER

One of the most difficult things we humans ever do is to be vulnerable. We have to admit that unless we allow others to be a part of our hearts, we are not fully alive.

22 NOVEMBER

Gratitude is demonstrated, not talked about.

23 NOVEMBER

Honor your original intentionality, stay in the moment, love in the moment, and ready yourself to be of maximum service to everyone who crosses your path.

24 NOVEMBER

Each day, I put a spiritual stake in the ground ahead of me and do my best to move toward it.

Thinking of you, Shannon Klenk

25 NOVEMBER

"Life is not life without love, it's merely existence, and if we're open, we can find love in everything," trumpeted the swan.

26 NOVEMBER

Knowledge wants to talk. Wisdom wants to listen. Hmmm, let me think about that.

27 NOVEMBER

May today be the most beautiful and amazing day of your life, and tomorrow, and the day after that, and the day after that. Get the picture?

28 NOVEMBER

"As long as you are passionately creating joyful creations, you will be on the planet creating and creating and creating!" giggled the otter.

29 NOVEMBER

I am love. So are you. It injures my spirit to forget that even for a moment.

30 NOVEMBER

Here's a thought from Mark Twain: "I was made merely in the image of God, but not otherwise enough to be mistaken for him by anybody but a very nearsighted person."

december

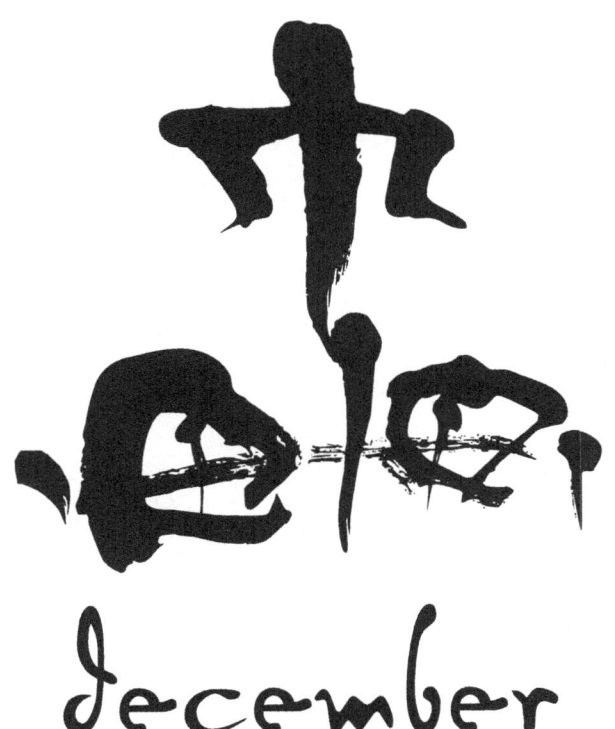

1 DECEMBER

Today, I am aware of how powerful my beliefs, thoughts, and emotions are in healing the world with love, literally and figuratively.

Thinking of you, Marilyn Horne & Janice Barnes

2 DECEMBER

I have lived through many terrible situations in my life, and some of them have actually happened.

3 DECEMBER

Today, I choose to live in an abundance of creativity, good health, and love.

4 DECEMBER

Hear the music in raindrops and the sound of sunlight and the secret whispers of the rocks and trees. This is the you who remembers that magic is at the heart of the world.

5 DECEMBER

Energy is powered by the grace of love. And, everything is energy.

6 DECEMBER

We may have different religious beliefs, but our faith abides in the same omnipotent presence. When we light our flames together, we banish darkness from the world.

7 DECEMBER

"Be tolerant of the people who are lost on their path. Ignorance, jealousy, anger, and greed stem from a lost soul. Pray that they'll find guidance."
~Native American Code of Ethics, 1994

8 DECEMBER

No one can steal your magic today. Embrace it, and show it to the world!

9 DECEMBER

Vulnerability may be the pathway to joy, but for most of us, it's a scary journey.

10 DECEMBER

Love who you are, not what you do.

11 DECEMBER

The smallest kindness done is much better than the grandest plans for great deeds. Act now. Quash negativity and evil in this world like a kindly, swashbuckling, sword-wielding lunatic! Start right where you are.

12 DECEMBER

The colossal misunderstanding of our time is the assumption that insight will work with people who are unmotivated to change.

13 DECEMBER

All of us on the planet need to be nurtured. It encourages our souls to flourish and express our creativity.

14 DECEMBER

That which you inspire today will impact the world tomorrow.

15 DECEMBER

Many of us are dazzled by shiny things ~ and an easier, softer way always looks shiny.

16 DECEMBER

When you have no place else to go, you realize that you are exactly where you are suppose to be.

17 DECEMBER

Appreciate the little things in your life. Then you will have joy in your heart and peace in your soul, today and always!

18 DECEMBER

Sometimes, to find the answers, you just need to look into your own heart.

19 DECEMBER

Preserving your ancestral history appears to be a noble act until you realize that it's often done at the expense of the future. So, be in the moment!

20 DECEMBER

The voice of untruth tells you, "These are really hard times." But the truth is, it's your opportunity to flourish in a new direction.

21 DECEMBER

Even the choicest words lose their power when they are used to dominate or control. Attitudes are the real figures of speech. So, I pause. What are my motives? What is the energy behind my words? If my motive is to serve and my energy is loving, I will be heard.

22 DECEMBER

Today, be the proof of the power of love, of believing in your dreams, and of doing the do. Be of service to everyone who crosses your path.

23 DECEMBER

Before you judge anything in your life, remember, God spins everything into gold!

24 DECEMBER

I believe true love allows us to be our authentic selves, to live in our original intentionality. Without it, something is lost. So many corny things have been written about love ~ love completes me and the like. But the truth is, we are love, so we're already complete.

25 DECEMBER

When we see joy in the eyes of those we love, we know it is the reflection of the God within us looking back at us and smiling.

26 DECEMBER

The only gift we can genuinely give to another is a part of ourselves. Now that's worth remembering!

27 DECEMBER

When we are apart, it makes me happy to think about seeing you again.

Missing you, Deirdre Mackey & Grace

28 DECEMBER

The essence, the energy, is and always will be. It cannot be expanded nor destroyed. It exists in form and out of form. It is the wind on our faces, the clouds in the sky, and the Earth that we feel under our feet. It is the fabric of all things ~ the trees, the flowers, the people we love, and those we have yet to meet. Breathe it in and embrace each moment.

29 DECEMBER

Love becomes real when you do something with it.

Thinking of you, Stephanie Schott

30 DECEMBER

Today, take one step toward moving the mountain that's keeping you from your dreams.

31 DECEMBER

"When all is said and done, we're all just walking each other home."

~Ram Dass

january

1 JANUARY

Every day we live on Earth is precious. Some people never realize this truth, but for those who do, it is an awesome journey!

2 JANUARY

What's keeping you from your dreams? Propel yourself into the day. Open your eyes, and thank God for another day. Then, launch yourself out of bed and into action before your brain can discourage you.

3 JANUARY

"Humankind has not woven the web of life. We are but one thread within it. Whatever we do to the web, we do to ourselves."
~Chief Seattle, 1854

4 JANUARY

We each have our story and life is about moving our story forward. When I answer these questions honestly, I stay on my path. What sparks my joy? What is my creation? What is my soul here to accomplish? How can I be of maximum service?

5 JANUARY

Focus on thoughts that make you feel good today. This allows every cell in your body to realign with its natural balance.

6 JANUARY

"There are times when I have no idea what comes next & it's the thing I've come to love most about being alive ~ leaning in to hear the invitation of each day & feeling my whole body melt when I say yes, yes, yes."

~ StoryPeople

7 JANUARY

When you live in spirit, you live in freedom.

8 JANUARY

Fear is a corroding threat to humanity. Remember this before you act in anger because behind all anger is fear.

9 JANUARY

God is the king of recycling. What I think is trash, he recycles for the highest good of all concerned.

10 JANUARY

You know that stubborn streak that keeps you from asking for help? Push it aside, and accept the grace and care God puts in your path from those who love you.

11 JANUARY

Today, do not be a victim in someone else's drama. Hmmm, the only way I can do that is through Love.

12 JANUARY

After we pray for direction, we must take action to do our part if there is to be permanent change.

Thinking of you, Kaycee Parker

13 JANUARY

Today, embrace your God-given potential to love tenderly, to walk humbly, and to serve others joyfully.

14 JANUARY

It's time to heal the broken heart of our Mother Earth. Since everything vibrates as energy, we begin by showing our love and care to everyone who crosses our path. Out of our conscious caring, we then pay attention to every sunrise, tree, stone, flower, and bird song.

15 JANUARY

Our spoken words carry great power. They can incite love or hatred, peace or civil disobedience, tenderness or cruelty. So today, I will speak joy; I will speak love.

16 JANUARY

Today, just show up without an expectation of being the star of the show or the center of attention. Just show up and be.

17 JANUARY

Some stranger, somewhere, still remembers you because you were kind to him when no one else was.

18 JANUARY

Father, grant me the heart of a grateful servant.

20 JANUARY

As we grow in the understanding of our spiritual essence, we see that we're made of God stuff. Period!

21 JANUARY

What's troubling you today? Is it really your burden? Sometimes, it's better to release your concerns for others rather than make them your own.

22 JANUARY

Our shared stories build the bridges that heal our hearts and bring us together.

23 JANUARY

"Today, take action. Follow through with what life puts in front of you. Action is what makes the creativity become visible," bellowed the bear.

24 JANUARY

Some doors only open from the inside. Embrace that thought today.

Thinking of you, Michel Reed

25 JANUARY

Breathe deeply, and feel the loving energy of Spirit fill you. Now, spread the love. Believe me, it matters.

26 JANUARY

Today, choose love to be the gift you give yourself!

27 JANUARY

The only place we truly communicate with another human being is through our experiences. That's where authentic wisdom is found.

28 JANUARY

Believe in your ability to do great things. Then, begin! Remember, amateurs built Noah's ark, and professionals built the Titanic.

29 JANUARY

Communication does not depend on syntax, or eloquence, or rhetoric, or articulation, but rather on the emotional context with which the message is being heard. Remember this before you open your mouth.

30 JANUARY

Frantic activity is not action! Ponder that for a moment.

31 JANUARY

Using a human solution for a spiritual malady never works. Only God can heal a spiritual malady. Remember this when you are trying to fix someone you cannot fix.

february

1 FEBRUARY

"If you have been brutally broken, but still have the courage to be gentle to other living beings, then you're a badass with the heart of an angel."

~Keanu Reeves

Thinking of you, Heather Lentz

2 FEBRUARY

See the light in your soul, the grace in your heart, and the energy within you. You are the swirling illumination of the Universe.

3 FEBRUARY

"The first time her laughter unfurled its wings in the wind, we knew that the world would never be the same."

~StoryPeople

Happy Birthday, Maddy!

4 FEBRUARY

A healthy relationship depends on asking for what you want, stating your intentions, and clearly understanding the intentions of the other person.

5 FEBRUARY

Be in love with exactly where you are today. Be in love with living in this moment.

Thinking of you, Liz Archibald

6 FEBRUARY

Create your life today by deliberate design and enthusiastic affirmations.

7 FEBRUARY

Perhaps the secret to longevity is to feel safe enough to stay curious. Hmmm, give that some thought.

8 FEBRUARY

What does a parent do when his child says, "I hate you." He says, "That's too bad because I love you, and there's nothing you can do about it." Hmmm. That's what God has said to me over and over and over again until I could see and embrace his eternal love for me, now and always.

Thinking of you, Marty Jeffery

9 FEBRUARY

Love is an action. It erases the scar tissue of the past.

10 FEBRUARY

Today, open the door for the love essence to come in. Remember, there is only a doorknob on your side of the door because the love is always there.

Thinking of you, Janet Finn

11 FEBRUARY

Today, picture what you want to be on the other side of crazy. Now, be that!

12 FEBRUARY

"All things seek to be reminded of what they are. If they are reminded enough, they can expand outward and become more. If they are reminded too much, they never become more. And if they are not reminded enough they, become scattered and vacant," whispered the willow tree.

13 FEBRUARY

It has been said that "Acceptance is the key to all my dilemmas." Hmm, I'll think about this today as I let go, so I don't have to be dragged.

14 FEBRUARY

Love is like a massive shockwave of multicolored light that comes from my chest, explodes out, and connects me to something much greater than myself.

15 FEBRUARY

In reviewing my intimate relationships, I realize that I became a reflection of who I thought my partner wanted me to be. I was afraid to be who I truly am because I believed the real me was not enough. Today, I chose to be my authentic self and let the chips fall where they may.

16 FEBRUARY

"Our first teacher is our own heart."
~Cheyenne proverb

Happy Birthday, Annette DiSabato

17 FEBRUARY

I am beginning to understand the power of thoughts. When I think it, I become it, whether I act on the thought or not.

18 FEBRUARY

When you practice being kind, it becomes a habit. When you practice being unkind, it becomes a habit. So what are you practicing?

19 FEBRUARY

The only thing worse than what I perceive as my difficulties is when I think I have the solutions to them.

20 FEBRUARY

Most of life is a process. Remember this the next time you're impatiently waiting for a solution that takes time to unfold.

21 FEBRUARY

Children are the seeds of our future. You need to plant love in their hearts and shower them with wisdom and precious life lessons. When they're grown, give them space to mature.

Happy Birthday, Aiden Spires

22 FEBRUARY

"When you are impeccably taking the steps upon a path that is truly yours, you will be on the path that is your essence," gurgled the babbling brook.

23 FEBRUARY

Joy is not the absence of pain, but the presence of God.

24 FEBRUARY

Who told you, "You can handle it?" No, you can't, and moreover, you don't have to. There is a humanity waiting to welcome you, support you, and help you heal. So today say, "I choose to open my heart and embrace the love of those wanting to help me."

25 FEBRUARY

Pride always stands in the way of my ability to forgive; and without forgiveness, there is no spiritual growth.

26 FEBRUARY

Listen to the whisper of God. He is saying to each of us that it's time to rekindle the love which he has put deep in our hearts, and bring it forth to serve others.

27 FEBRUARY

"You must be joined with the energy of all beings on Earth if you are to have a perception of prosperity," bellowed the buffalo.

28 FEBRUARY

When passion moves you to action, your desires become reality.

29 FEBRUARY

Over the years, I have read many books with thoughts for the day, and I always felt cheated on Leap Year because there was no February 29. Was I supposed to reread February 28 again? Was I supposed to skip a day? Now, you have something to read today. You can even read February 29 on the years that do not have a Leap Year.

Self-reflection will be distorted until and unless I unplug from my unconscious mind and plug into the infinite energy of the divine.

march

1 MARCH

Why does it take so long to find our way home to who we really are? We want to say, "It ain't so." And for a rare handful, that may be true. But most of us wander around pretending we know ourselves, and we are nothing more than a reflection of who we think others want us to be. To be the real me requires vulnerability. Today, I will be vulnerable to everyone I meet and in return, I will be me.

2 MARCH

Life is about doing rather than trying. So, be sure the people in your life encourage what you are doing. Otherwise, you will continue to "try" and be standing still forever.

3 MARCH

It's not what you listen to that matters, it's what you can hear.

4 MARCH

Living in the light is more than a saying! We don't let in the light, we are the light. Whether it's light or energy or love, it's all the same stuff. Now wrap your head around that because it's the truth.

Happy Birthday, Dad!

5 MARCH

Swim in God today. Submerge yourself and just be. Float in the Holy Water. Feel the love, peace, and serenity that comes with God's grace.

6 MARCH

"Art is the creative force of the person creating it. Technology is the means by which one creates. And so by definition, there can be no separation of the two."

Well said, Jason Carey.

7 MARCH

"Never let the hardship of the journey overshadow the glory of reaching your destination," whispered the Essence.

8 MARCH

"Luck is where preparation meets opportunity."

~Randy Pausch

9 MARCH

Realize your convictions and follow them passionately. Do not be persuaded by others to follow their passions instead of your own.

10 MARCH

Today, praise God for all of his wisdom that you understand and all that you do not.

11 MARCH

Being vulnerable is the doorway to joy. We can no longer hide from the truth of who we are. We must push through the fear and trust that what lies ahead is beyond our wildest imaginings.

12 MARCH

For me, writing is art created out of the English language. It is my passion, the thing I must do. So what is your passion, the thing you must do? Do that today!

13 MARCH

"Some pursue happiness; others create it."
~Unknown

Thinking of you, Mark Mathews

14 MARCH

"It would not be much of a Universe if it wasn't home to the people you love."
~Stephen Hawking

15 MARCH

Do not define your soul by the shell it's in at the moment!

16 MARCH

Whatever is in front of you to accomplish, know this: Once you become willing to do it, the how will be revealed.

17 MARCH

Someone said you have to be Irish to celebrate St. Patty's Day. Well, here's a news flash: We're all made of the same stuff, so we're all Irish, and we're everything else, too.

Happy St. Patty's Day!

18 MARCH

"Don't take what isn't yours either from a person, community, or culture. It wasn't earned nor given. It isn't yours."
~Native American Code of Ethics, 1994

19 MARCH

Kindness has so much more power than you can even imagine. Remember this as you go through the day.

20 MARCH

"Impossible is just a big word thrown around by small men who find it easier to live in the world they've been given than to explore the power they have to change it. Impossible is not a fact. It's an opinion. Impossible is not a declaration. It's a dare. Impossible is potential. Impossible is temporary. Impossible is nothing."
~Muhammad Ali

21 MARCH

When I allow anyone or anything to rent space in my head, there's no room for new creations to be born.

22 MARCH

I have an essence and a value that are greater than any material condition in my life. God loves me big and is caring for me in this moment and the next moment and every moment.

23 MARCH

If the Holy Mother, Mary, was walking among us today, I believe she would say: "What is your purpose for being on the planet right now? If it's anything beside serving others with love, think again."

Happy Birthday, Jesse Pope

24 MARCH

"Standing Together" is a powerful battlecry that can restore the dignity of America.

Thinking of you, Mike Horne

25 MARCH

Today, may you melt into the center of your longing.

26 MARCH

"No nation deserves to exist if it permits itself to lose stern and virile virtues, and this without regard to whether the loss is due to the growth of a heartless and all-absorbing commercialism, to prolonged indulgence in luxury and soft, effortless ease, or to the deification of a warped and twisted sentimentality."
~President Theodore Roosevelt, August 1910

27 MARCH

If everyone felt loved and inspired, there would be no more fear or pain in this world. Oh wait, we are love, so feel inspired.

28 MARCH

"Guilt is a direct result of thinking you had a power that you didn't have in that moment," said the badger.

29 MARCH

Sometimes standing still is the only way to figure out which way to go.

30 MARCH

Deepen your spiritual connection today. Breathe in the Love of the Essence, and feel it's cleansing water flow over you! All is well!

31 MARCH

"Naturally magnanimous and open-minded, the red man prefers to believe that the Spirit of God is not breathed into man alone, but that the whole created Universe is a sharer in the immortal perfection of its Maker."
~Jack Red Cloud, Oglala Lakota

april

1 APRIL

Today, take time to laugh because it's the music of the soul.

2 APRIL

When I change my thinking, my world changes. This is true no matter what I'm thinking. Hmmm, let me think about that.

3 APRIL

Be reminded of the miracles in your life today by seeing the miracles in the lives of others.

4 APRIL

Having everything is when you have nothing and no one can take it away from you.

5 APRIL

Be committed to thrive today and tomorrow and the day after that!

6 APRIL

God is not preparing a blessing for you; God is preparing you for a blessing.

7 APRIL

"The noblest art is that of making others happy."

~P. T. Barnum

8 APRIL

When I am stuck in the pain of betrayal, I'm moving away from God.

9 APRIL

When my niece, Jenny Rebecca, was a little girl, there was a family tragedy that caused her confusion and sadness. There was one person I knew would have an answer for her. It was Mother Angelica who founded the Eternal Word Television Network in Birmingham, Alabama. Mother Angelica held Jenny on her lap and said, "Even though you're sad, know that your parents love you, your Aunt Nan loves you, I love you, and Jesus loves you. But when you don't feel the love inside, just knowing will be enough." So today I say to you:

"Know that you are dearly loved, and when you don't feel the love inside, just knowing will be enough."

10 APRIL

Hey, just for today, don't push the river. (It flows by itself.)

11 APRIL

Today, unleash your boundless potential ~ mentally, emotionally, spiritually. You are the creator of your joy and your destiny.

Thinking of you, Jesse Lentz

12 APRIL

When I'm not okay with me, I make you wrong. Think about it.

13 APRIL

Faith is always being thankful. It is knowing that no matter what happens, God will use it for our highest good.

14 APRIL

Today remember, you are a jewel in God's crown.

Happy Birthday, Carole Pope

15 APRIL

"It is not necessary to believe in God to be a good person. In a way, the traditional notion of God is outdated. One can be spiritual but not religious. It is not necessary to go to church and give money. For many, nature can be a church. Some of the best people in history did not believe in God, while some of the worst deeds were done in His name."

~Pope Francis

16 APRIL

"I carry you with me into the world, into the smell of rain & the words that dance between people & for me, it will always be this way, walking in the light, remembering being alive together."

~StoryPeople

Leslie John Rafferty, I miss you still.

17 APRIL

"All of life is a process, not an event." Who said that?

18 APRIL

The most important property of energy is that it is perpetuated ~ it does not change with time. This is known as the law of conservation of energy. It will always be energy, even if it changes form. So today, lean into the energy of love.

19 APRIL

The power of our words will heal us or hurt us. So what are you speaking into existence today, self-blaming or self-blessing?

20 APRIL

"Nature is not for us, but rather a part of us. Animals, plants, and all living creatures are part of our worldly family."
~Native American Code of Ethics, 1994

21 APRIL

When did the world change from honoring the Earth to considering it a commodity?

22 APRIL

"Stop worrying about Mother Earth because she will take care of herself," the turtle said. "Start worrying about yourselves because when Mother Earth has had enough, she will shake you humans off the planet like little ants."

Happy Earth Day

23 APRIL

"It is not the critic who counts; not the man who points out how the strong man stumbles, or where the doer of deeds could have done them better. The credit belongs to the man who is actually in the arena, whose face is marred by dust and sweat and blood; who strives valiantly; who errs, who comes short again and again, because there is no effort without error and shortcoming; but who does actually strive to do the deeds; who knows great enthusiasms, the great devotions; who spends himself in a worthy cause; who at the best knows in the end the

triumph of high achievement, and who at the worst, if he fails, at least fails while daring greatly, so that his place shall never be with those cold and timid souls who neither know victory nor defeat."
~President Theodore Roosevelt

24 APRIL

"You cannot get through a single day without having an impact on the world around you. What you do makes a difference, and you have to decide what kind of a difference you want to make."
~Jane Goodall

25 APRIL

Our voices speak to the Universe; our written words speak to our souls.

26 APRIL

Today, amazing things await you. Embrace them, stay focused, and take action in the unfolding.

27 APRIL

Today, don't treat a stranger better than you treat yourself.

Thinking of you, Bert Wright

28 APRIL

"It's easier to fool people than to convince them that they have been fooled."
~Mark Twain

29 APRIL

If your life is full of blessings, it's because you are a blessing, and vice-versa.

Thinking of you, Dan Dever

30 APRIL

"All I can tell you is there is a moment where you finally stop & refuse to pretend this life is not yours & suddenly being strong looks a lot like laughing & crying & dancing & listening deeply to the people you love, & now & then you'll look back at that old way & wonder how you ever believed that life was something to endure."
~StoryPeople

Happy Arbor Day

Thinking of you, Marty Jeffery

may

1 MAY

"The land was put here for us by the Great Spirit, and we cannot sell it because it does not belong to us. You can count your money and burn it within the nod of a buffalo's head, but only Great Spirit can count the grains of sand and the blades of grass of these plains. As a present to you, we will give you anything we have that you can take with you, but the land, NEVER."
~Two Guns, Blackfoot Chief

2 MAY

Life is meant to be lived, not analyzed. Think about it.

3 MAY

Today, I will stay in touch with my spiritual center. This is where I find the courage for another day.

4 MAY

We live in a society that says, "Accept it and move on." That injures our spirits. We have to feel it, grieve it, and understand it. Only then can we truly go through it and move on to the light.

5 MAY

"Be Love ~ so much love that when others are with you, they are love, too."

~Ram Dass

6 MAY

When Mother Nature speaks, quiet yourself enough to pay attention to her story.

7 MAY

Know that you are here by choice to be part of the great awakening. Honor your truth, and be humbled by your magnificence.

Message to my heart from Great Spirit

8 MAY

In the land of darkness, the light within shines brightest.

9 MAY

God lives in the moment and he lives in you and me. That's where I find him. So, in order to have a life of love, joy, and peace, I must have a conscious contact with God and ask: "What would you have me do in this moment?" I'll do that today.

Thinking of you, Susan Struebing

10 MAY

Today, bench press the weight of your own imagination.

11 MAY

Focus on feeling your desire, regardless of the chaos that surrounds you. Make this a daily practice. Then, watch your life change.

12 MAY

Today, feel like you already have whatever it is you want in your life ~ love, joy, laughter ~ because you do.

13 MAY

I always say a prayer before I write anything. God is the author, and I am his scribe.

14 MAY

Have you ever thought, "I can tell he's judgmental just by looking at him." I have and that's a judgement. Just for today, I'll stop judging others. And then do it again tomorrow and the day after and the day after that. Are you getting the idea?

15 MAY

My friend, Steve Szabo, shares his daily prayer: "Dear God, my actions today are my prayer to you. Please guide me to do what you would have me do, see what you would have me see, hear what you would have me hear, and speak what you would have me speak. And thank you for giving me the juice to do your will always."

16 MAY

Living gives us the experience to see situations differently. There really are no shortcuts.

17 MAY

"Search for yourself, by yourself. Do not allow others to create your path for you. It's your road and yours alone. Others might walk it with you, but no one can walk it for you."
~Native American Code of Ethics, 1994

18 MAY

The spiritual life is not a theory; we must live it one day at a time.

19 MAY

Be the light in someone's darkness; it will heal you both.

20 MAY

God can help the crazy, but not the unwilling.

21 MAY

"The soul continues to exist through all our many lifetimes. It never, ever abandons us. Our souls have greater faith in us than we do in them. There is no judgement, only joy," whispered the wind.

22 MAY

When chasing your passion, the most dangerous "no" you can ever hear is the "no" you tell yourself. So today, just say "yes" to doing the next thing and tomorrow, just say "yes," and every day, just say "yes." Watch your life change!

23 MAY

The internet lacks a librarian to sort and separate the fiction from the non-fiction. Remember this before you read someone's opinion about the truth as a fact rather than fiction.

24 MAY

In order to know the depths of kindness and love, you must also know the deepest sorrow.

25 MAY

There is a wonderful mythical law of nature which is that the things we crave most in life ~ love, happiness, freedom, and peace of mind ~ are always attained by giving them to someone else.

Thinking of you, Vikki Rood

26 MAY

Have you ever thought about the fact that we ask for God's help and then we want to dictate how he gives it? Today, accept the help that God brings your way. He knows lots more about what's best for you than you do.

27 MAY

When doors shut along life's journey, look for open windows!

28 MAY

In any given moment, you are either in conscious connection with God and humanity or in conscious separation from God and humanity. There is no middle ground. So today, be vigilant to stay connected.

29 MAY

What kind of footprint did you leave on our planet today? Think about it.

30 MAY

All of life is about going through whatever lies ahead rather than getting over it.

31 MAY

I realize that the longer I am on the planet, the less important it is for people to know that I am here. I matter. And so do you and you and you. But being the center of attention is no longer my motive. It's better for me to be in a neutral space that allows those around me to shine.

june

1 JUNE

"There's much more in any given moment than we perceive, and we, ourselves, are much more than we perceive. When you know that, part of you can stand outside the drama of your life."

~Ram Dass

2 JUNE

Watch for the animals you see around you today. This is a time when all the creatures on the planet are very close to us and are bringing us truth, love, and encouragement.

3 JUNE

Listen for the laughter! That's the presence of God.

4 JUNE

"They talk about angels, but what if the angels are within us, and all we need to do is unfold our wings."

~StoryPeople

5 JUNE

Free will is a funny thing. In any given lifetime, it so often keeps us from our destiny because we allow ourselves to be distracted. Decide today to use your free will to propel you toward your destiny. Focus on what you are here to do, and do it.

6 JUNE

Trust is falling into the wind knowing that God will be there to catch you.

7 JUNE

Sometimes a true friend will tell you what you do not what to hear. Listen, because it's coming from love.

8 JUNE

"Love flows. Love doesn't know boundaries. The mind creates boundaries. The mind creates the boundary of separate me and you. The heart just keeps embracing and opening out."
~Ram Dass

Thinking of you, Deidre Mackey

9 JUNE

You must have hope for your creativity to thrive.

10 JUNE

Have a Double D & E Day ~ Diet and Exercise, Discipline and Effort, Diet and Exercise, Discipline and Effort, Diet and Exercise, Discipline and Effort. Without these, you will have no place to live! Think about it.

11 JUNE

Today, do everything in moderation including moderation.

12 JUNE

"Everything you love will probably be lost, but in the end, love will return in a different way. Embrace the change. Together, we can turn pain into wonder and love, but it's up to us to make that connection consciously and intentionally."

~Franz Kafka (1883-1924)

Happy Birthday, Linda Lou Bradley

13 JUNE

Know that your heart has been cracked open, and you are learning to walk anew.

14 JUNE

Today, I will yield my will to God. I will trust that he will open me to new joys, awarenesses, and discoveries.

15 JUNE

"I have heard too much beauty to ever go back, he said, & in that moment, I knew there was no way the children of our world would fail."

~StoryPeople

Happy Birthday, Leo Spires

16 JUNE

"Know the river has its destination. The elders say we must let go of the shore, push off into the middle of the river, keep our eyes open, and our heads above water. And I say, See who is in there with you and celebrate."
~Hopi Elder, Oraibi, Arizona

17 JUNE

I look in the mirror each day as I leave the bathroom. God laughs, and reminds me I cannot even control my hair, let alone people, places, or things. I accept his invitation to go play. One day at a time, I show up for my life. It works.

18 JUNE

Listen to the whisper of the Creator. He is saying that it is time to rekindle that which you have put deep in your heart and bring it forth to serve others.

19 JUNE

Sometimes I can't see the good in me. That's when I need you to remind me of who I really am. It gives me the courage to move forward.

20 JUNE

Do something kind for yourself today. Do something kind for a stranger today. Do something kind for someone you love but who is also really upsetting you at the moment. Don't plan to do it, just do it. And don't keep score.

21 JUNE

"We fail to recognize what we can do until we can't do it," Bobbi Jo said.

Happy Birthday, Bobbi Jo Pope

22 JUNE

Stop trying to make others the same as you so you can feel safe. It blinds you to the strengths within your differences.

23 JUNE

There is no proof that Jesus was born in December. In fact, many theologians and scientists believe his birth occurred in the late spring or early summer. It is agreed that it occurred in Bethlehem. What if his birthday is June 23? We should have a celebration and spread joy and love today. Since we may never know for sure, we should have a celebration and spread joy and love everyday. Just sayin'

24 JUNE

Life is not about living forever ~ it's about making life count.

25 JUNE

"Remember, when life is tough, have a laugh. If you can laugh in the face of adversity, then you are bulletproof."
~Ricky Gervais

26 JUNE

Spiritual maladies cannot be fixed with intellectual solutions. Only the energy of love can heal a spiritual affliction.

27 JUNE

"Today is only one day in all the days that will ever be. But what will happen in all the other days that ever come can depend on what you do today."
~Ernest Hemingway

28 JUNE

Transformation occurs when we face our fears, so run toward them today.

29 JUNE

All the prayers in the world won't allow God into my heart if I hold on to resentments and whine about the actions of others.

Thinking of you, Katherine King

30 JUNE

Sometimes speaking the truth to someone who is not ready to hear it is like throwing a bucket against the wall. It makes a lot of noise, but it doesn't do any good

緑

july

1 JULY

"Let every nation know, whether it wishes us well or ill, that we shall pay any price, bear any burden, meet any hardship, support any friend, oppose any foe, in order to assure the survival and success of liberty."
~President John F. Kennedy

2 JULY

I believe we have all chosen to be on the planet right now. There are no coincidences. We do not change when we are comfortable, we change when we are uncomfortable. This has been true throughout human history. We have come to this point, and you are here to be part of it. Our power lies within us. We are spirits with skin to champion this new day.

3 JULY

"Nearly all men can stand adversity, but if you want to test a man's character, give him power."

~Abraham Lincoln

4 JULY

America is our foundation on which to build. The idea that we have lost our way is only the case if we believe it. All the power is within us, and that is the ideal of America.

5 JULY

"In America, change is possible. It's in our hands. Together, I know we'll get there. Look how far we've already come."

~President Barack Obama

6 JULY

Remember that everything, and that means everything, is energy. So, the reality is that no one is more or less, better or worse. Ponder that today.

7 JULY

Today, feel the wind dancing around you, and see the sparkles of stardust everywhere.

8 JULY

Sound vibration restores health. Sound vibration, moving through water, restores the soul. Allow yourself to feel this one.

9 JULY

If common sense was lard, most people wouldn't be able to grease a pan.

Happy Birthday, Hot Dog Nellie

10 JULY

A great leader comes from deeply held values, inherent humility, comportment of servility, and determination to create trust over chaos.

11 JULY

"Our aim is not to do away with corporations; on the contrary, these big aggregations are an inevitable development of modern industrialism. We are not hostile to them; we are merely determined that they shall be so handled as to subserve the public good. We draw the line against misconduct, not against wealth."
~President Theodore Roosevelt
December, 1902

12 JULY

As we come together, we restore the American Spirit because we are the American Spirit.

13 JULY

"In the end, we will remember not the words of our enemies, but the silence of our friends."
~Dr. Martin Luther King Jr.

14 JULY

Today, be a contributor on the wheel of humanity rather than a cog in it.

15 JULY

"While working men and women have long known the value of a dollar ~ it is a lesson well taught to one who labors for a living ~ it has taken a long, long time to teach employers the value of a human being."

~James Riddle Hoffa

16 JULY

God embraces me, flaws and all. He wants me to feel his love in each moment. So, I embrace this day with grace and joy and laughter, and experience all that life has to offer.

Happy Birthday, Grandma Grace

17 JULY

The things I allow to come to me are far greater than what I chase after on my own.

18 JULY

Whatever you're going through today, know this: God is making room in your heart for something new.

19 JULY

Today remember, meeting again after moments or lifetimes is certain for those who are friends.

20 JULY

"We've learned to fly the air like birds; we've learned to swim the seas like fish. So when will we learn to walk the Earth as brothers and sisters?"

~C.E.M. Joad, 1929

21 JULY

Written in the DNA of each soul on the planet is his or her authentic purpose. Even though outside circumstances may cloud the truth of who you really are, it is always within you. So today, look from the inside out, not the outside in.

22 JULY

Be present in your life today. Your life is real. The moments you spend being with loved ones, planting a flower, or saving a mouse is your real life. All the rest, the momentary life situations, is just mind stuff. What endures forever is your real life, and your real life is Love.

Happy Birthday, Cat Spires!

23 JULY

"Until the lion learns to write, every story will glorify the hunter."

~African Proverb

24 JULY

And one more thing:

You can never, ever, ever have too much glitter. I love you Big!

Now Start Again!

FINAL NOTE

I believe that as we moved out of the Piscean Age (Will and Power) into the Aquarian age (Love and Harmony), there was a natural energy shift. We were opened up to the ten dimensions. We moved into the fluidity of peace, love, and harmony. We moved out of hatred, greed, and control.

Although it may feel as though hatred still has a stronghold on humanity, it is really just the last gasping breath of a dying false belief system. It is a culture that puts money before people. It is a culture that puts blame on others rather than taking responsibility for the actions and consequences of self-serving greed.

The young ones will not live that way. They are making their voices heard right now saying, "No More!"

With the challenge of a worldwide pandemic, everyone on the planet has gotten to see what really matters in one's life. This great awakening has increased the love energy in ways we could never have imagined.

There is something so powerful that happens when one heart connects to another. That energy of love continues to thrive whether we meet again in moments or lifetimes. Wow! That's stunning.

The elders and young ones who understand and encourage peace, love, and harmony are leading the charge into a new world. But change can only occur when we know what needs to be changed. Clearly, this is a time when everyone has realized that words and actions have consequences.

Humanity will look back at this time sixty years from now and wonder how any of us could have lived in a world filled with cruelty and hatred. That's why it's a really good idea to stay healthy, so you will be here to see the return to total love.

ABOUT ME

I write stellar books! Novels, devotionals, cookbooks, kids' books, and screenplays. It's my passion, it's why I breathe. It's my service to humanity. I know the revealing power of words. Whether they are spoken or written, a single word can change the intended meaning.

My career path has included newspaper reporter, speech writer, and professor. I learned not only the power of words, but the importance of finding the facts.

I believe a printed page is a picture. Words have texture and energy as well as meaning. As the words come together, it's like a concerto being played by an orchestra. The tone and cadence, the crescendos, the de-crescendos become part of the fabric of the story.

So, as you read these daily affirmations, I encourage you to listen with your third ear. Pause and reflect. Allow the words to speak to your heart.

May your days be filled with love and blessings beyond measure.

~ND

ACKNOWLEDGEMENTS

A special thank you to Littel Industries for permission to use some of the wisdom of The Storyteller throughout this book.

28 July - Hopi Elder, Oraibi, Arizona. Public Domain.
1 August - Native American Code of Ethics, 1994. Public Domain.
11 August - Native American Proverb. Public Domain.
14 August - Ram Dass. Permission requested.
17 August - StoryPeople. Used with permission.
19 August - Crowfoot, Blackfoot Lakota. Public Domain.
21 August - StoryPeople. Used with permission.
25 August - US Senator John McCain. Public Domain.
31 August - Nassim Haramein. Permission requested Resonance Science Foundation.
3 September - Tim Cook, Apple CEO. Permission requested.
14 September - StoryPeople. Used with permission.
2 October - Hopi Elder, Oraibi, Arizona. Public Domain.
5 October - StoryPeople. Used with permission.
13 October - Marilyn Monroe. Permission requested.
23 October - Ram Dass. Permission requested.
28 October - StoryPeople. Used with permission.
18 November - Asaro Tribe, Papua, New Guinea. Public Domain.
30 November - Mark Twain. Public Domain.

7 December - Native American Code of Ethics, 1994. Public Domain.

31 December - Ram Dass. Permission requested.

3 January - Chief Seattle, 1854. Public Domain.

6 January - StoryPeople. Used with permission.

19 January - Dolly Parton. Permission requested.

1 February - Keanu Reeves. Permission requested.

3 February - StoryPeople. Used with permission.

16 February - Cheyenne proverb. Public Domain.

8 March - Randy Pausch. Permission requested.

14 March - Stephen Hawkins. Permission requested.

18 March - Native American Code of Ethics, 1994. Public Domain.

19 March - Muhammed Ali. Permission requested.

25 March - President Theodore Roosevelt, August 1910. Public Domain.

31 March - Jack Red Cloud, Oglala Lakota. Public Domain.

7 April - P. T. Barnum. Public Domain.

15 April - Pope Francis. Public Domain.

16 April - StoryPeople. Used with permission.

20 April - Native American Code of Ethics, 1994. Public Domain.

23 April - President Theodore Roosevelt. Excerpt from The Man in the Arena speech delivered at the Sorbonne in Paris, France, on 23 April 1910. Public Domain.

24 April - Jane Goodall. Permission requested.

28 April - Mark Twain. Public Domain.

30 April - StoryPeople. Used with permission.

1 May - Two Guns, Blackfoot Chief. Public Domain.

5 May - Ram Dass. Permission requested.

17 May - Native American Code of Ethics, 1994. Public Domain.
1 June - Ram Dass. Permission requested.
4 June - StoryPeople. Used with permission.
8 June - Ram Dass. Permission requested.
12 June - Franz Kafka (1883-1924). Public Domain.
15 June - StoryPeople. Used with permission.
16 June - Hopi Elder, Oraibi, Arizona. Public Domain.
25 June - Ricky Gervais. Permission requested.
27 June - Earnest Hemingway. Public Domain.
1 July - President John F. Kennedy. Public Domain.
3 July - President Abraham Lincoln. Public Domain.
5 July - President Barack Obama. Public Domain.
11 July - President Theodore Roosevelt, 1902. Public Domain.
13 July - Dr. Martin Luther King Jr. Public Domain.
15 July - James Riddle Hoffa. Public Domain.
20 July - C.E.M. Joad, 1929. Public Domain.
23 July - African Proverb. Public Domain.

We have made every effort to contact the appropriate sources of these attributions. If we have overlooked giving proper credit to anyone, please accept our apology. Should any discrepancies be found, the publisher welcomes any written documentation supporting the correction for future publications.

Made in the USA
Monee, IL
10 July 2022